"Good morning, Mommy! Can we make breakfast together?"
"Of course," Mommy said warmly.

Mommy gently combs Little bear's hair.
"I like this little flower"

" Mommy, what should I do?"
" Mommy teaches you, take your time." Mommy encourages her.

Mommy taught her how to stir the honey and pour milk.

They had breakfast together. Honey touched her nose, making Mommy laugh.

Later, they walked the meadow. Mommy showed her how to smell flowers.

A bee buzzed near. She felt scared.
Mommy held her paw gently.
“Don’ t worry. I’ m here,” said Mommy. And Little Bear felt safe

They sat in the meadow weaving a daisy crown.
"For you, Mommy," Little Bearsaid.
"It suits the kindest queen I know."
again.

Mommy hugged the Little bear, butterflies and gentle sunshine surrounded them.

In the afternoon, they baked cookies. The sweet smell filled the room.

The cookies were baked, Little bear leaned against Mommy to watch TV.
She tasted one. “It’ s yummy, Mommy!”

At the table they mixed berry colors and painted side by side. Mommy drew a big heart.

Little bear drew Mommy's appearance on paper and imagined her smiling face in her mind.

At night, Mommy knitted a scarf by the fireplace,Little bear played with toys beside Mommy.
"Mommy, it's time to tell stories!"

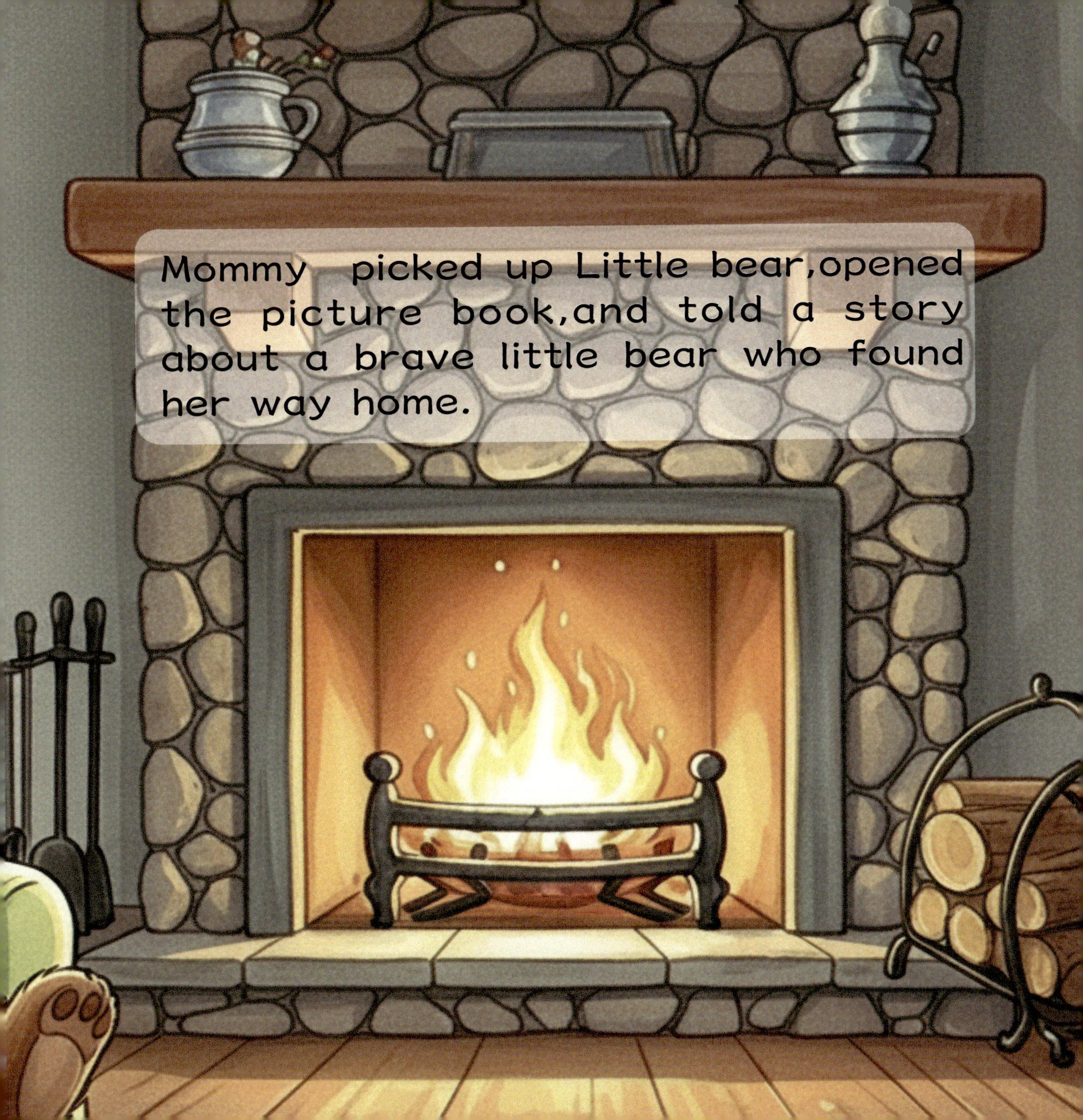

Mommy picked up Little bear,opened the picture book,and told a story about a brave little bear who found her way home.

As the stars shone,she fell into a sweet dream.

Mommy whispered, “I’ ll always protect you.”